MEET THE FAMILY

"Hello, I am Daddy Square"

"Hello everybody, I am Mummy Circle"

"Hiya! I am Lucy Oval"

"I hope you enjoy our book. I am Daisy Heart"

"Nice to meet you, I am Johnny Star"

Copyright © Monika & Lawrence 2018. All rights reserved.
Family Shapes™ is a registered trademark.

Author: Monika & Lawrence.
Book Illustrators: Kirsten Martin McKenzie/Tina Wijesir.
Characters designed by Mary Ibeh.

No part of this book may be reproduced in any form or by any means, electronic or mechanical, including information storage and retrieval systems, without permission in writing from the author. The only exception is by a reviewer, who may quote short excerpts in a review.

This book is a work of fiction. Names, characters, places, and incidents either are products of the authors' imagination or are used fictitiously. Any resemblance to actual persons, living or dead, events, or locales is entirely coincidental.

It is the reader's responsibility to determine the value and quality of any recipe or instructions provided for food preparation and to determine the nutritional value if any, as well as the safety of the preparation instructions.

The recipe presented is intended for entertainment and/or informational purposes and for use by persons having the appropriate technical skill, at their own risk.

First printing July 2018

ISBN-978-1-9164012-1-1

enquries@familyshapes.co.uk
@familyshapes
www.familyshapes.co.uk
Facebook : Family Shapes

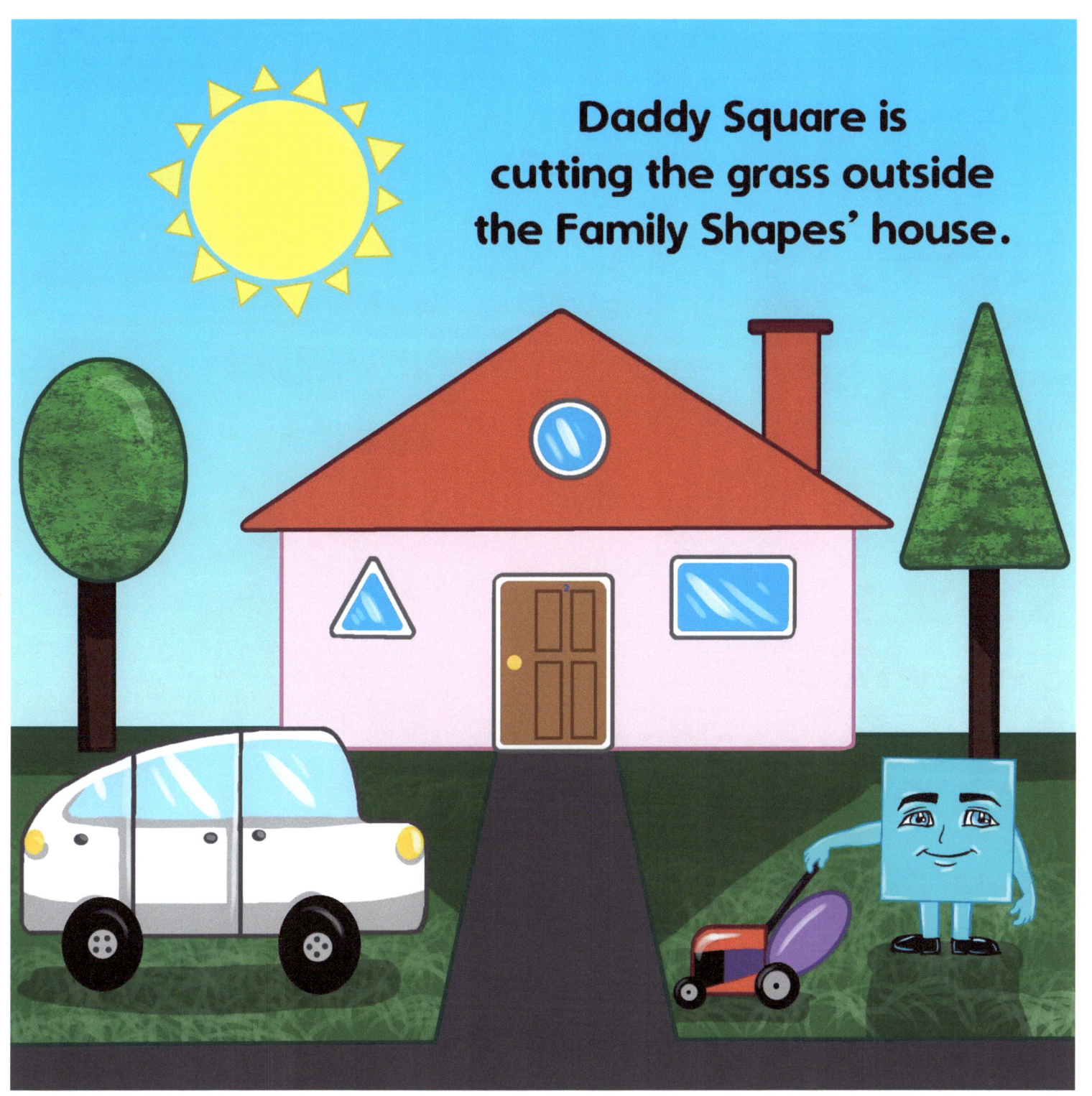

Mummy Circle and her three children, Johnny Star, Lucy Oval, and Daisy Heart are in their kitchen.

They have decided to make cookies.

Mummy Circle is preparing the table.

Family Shapes will need: flour, sugar, butter, an egg, vanilla, a mixing bowl, a spoon, a rolling pin and a sieve.

Mummy Circle is mixing the ingredients.

Mummy Circle is rolling the dough.

Lucy Oval is getting the shape cutters ready.

Johnny Star is cutting rectangle-shaped cookies.

Lucy Oval is cutting square-shaped cookies.

Mummy Circle is cutting diamond-shaped cookies.

Daisy Heart is cutting triangle-shaped cookies.

The children
are putting
the shaped cookies
on the tray.

Mummy Circle is putting the cookies in the oven.

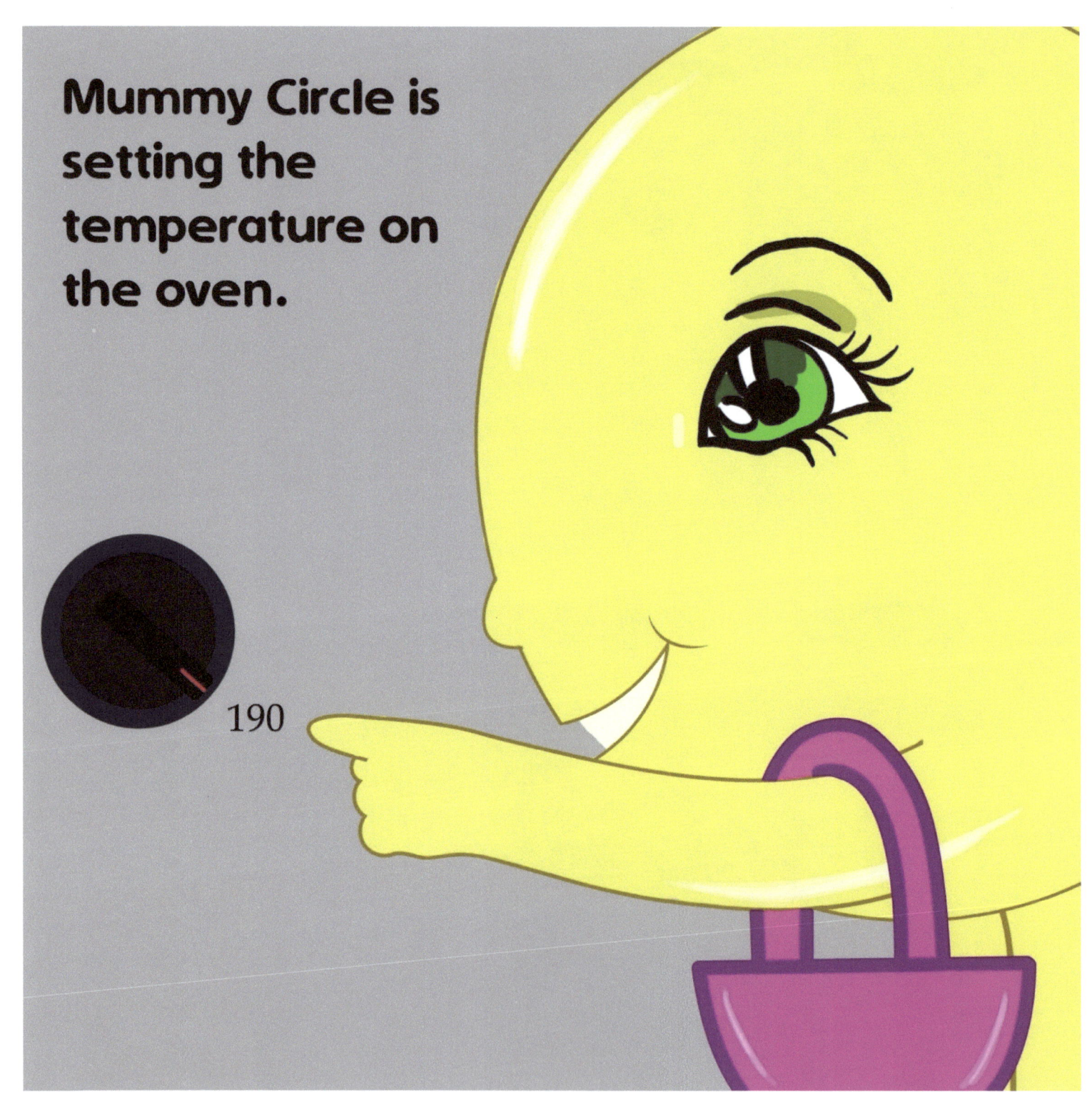

Johnny Star is putting the spoon in the sink.

Daisy Heart is licking the bowl.

The children are wiping the table and Mummy Circle is washing up.

Lucy Oval is very excited, "Mummy, Mummy, when will the cookies be ready?"

Mummy Circle says, "In about 8-12 minutes."

The children are getting excited as Mummy Circle is taking the shaped cookies out of the oven.

Daddy Square has finished cutting the grass and has come inside. "Something smells lovely," says Daddy.

Family Shapes are enjoyin

g their delicious cookies.

Johnny Star says, "These cookies are yummy!" Daddy and Johnny 'high-five' each other.

The End.

Or is it?

Interactive Questions

* Who is your favourite Family Shapes character and why?
* What shapes can you see on the page where Daddy Square is cutting the grass?
* What were the shapes of the cookies?
* What shapes can you see around you?
* Can you draw the shapes of the family and name them.
* Ask a grown-up if they can help you make Family Shapes cookies.

Family Shapes™ Cookies Recipe

Preparation time : 30 minutes
Cooking time : 8-12 minutes
Makes approximately 20 cookies

Ingredients :
160g Softened butter (approx 3/4 cup)
160g Caster sugar (approx 3/4 cup)
310g All-purpose flour (approx 2 cups)
1 Large egg
1 tsp of Vanilla extract.

Please try and involve the children as much as possible when making your Family Shapes cookies.

Lightly butter the baking tray - or you can use greaseproof paper.
Cream together the butter and the sugar until its light and fluffy, then add the egg and vanilla and continue to beat.
Sieve and stir in the flour and mix well until the mixture binds into a soft dough. Place the dough in the fridge for 20 minutes-or a little longer if you can.
Place the mixture on a floured surface and gently roll out to about 1/8 of an inch thick-or your preferred thickness.
Use your cookie cutters to cut out the shapes then transfer them onto the baking tray.
Preheat oven to 190° C / 375° F / Gas 5.
Bake in the oven for approximately 8-12 minutes until they are about to turn golden brown on the edges. Set aside to cool.

Enjoy your Family Shapes Cookies!

www.ingramcontent.com/pod-product-compliance
Lightning Source LLC
Chambersburg PA
CBHW041227040426
42444CB00002B/85